EXPLORE THE WILD WEST

PIONEER EDITION

By Brian LaFleur and Shirleyann Costigan

CONTENTS

Forgotten
COWBOYS

African American cowboys were tough. They were brave. A few even became famous. Yet history forgot them for many years.

✦ By Brian LaFleur ✦

In the Old American West, cowboys had a tough job. They moved big groups of **cattle** over long distances. They also tamed wild horses. Their lives were exciting and dangerous.

About 100,000 people worked as cowboys. A lot were white. But many cowboys were African Americans.

After the **Civil War**, many African Americans moved west to find better lives. But they experienced **discrimination**, or unequal treatment. Often they could only find the hardest and most dangerous jobs. That's why many became cowboys.

Because cowboys were brave, some became famous. Writers wrote books about them. Some cowboys wrote books about themselves.

Nat Love wrote a famous cowboy book about himself in 1907. In his book, Love told stories about his amazing life. The book became very popular.

Love did not start life as a cowboy. He was born as an enslaved person in Tennessee in 1854. When the Civil War ended and he was freed, Love wanted to go to school. But he could not find one. So when he was fifteen years old, he headed west.

Nat Love. *He loved "the wild and free life of the plains."*

Bill Pickett. *This rodeo star was the first to jump onto a steer and wrestle it to the ground.*

4

A Young Man Goes West

Love moved to Dodge City, Kansas. There he got a job as a cowboy. The job paid $30 a month. He became well-known for his skills with horses.

Love wrote about taking cattle from Texas to Kansas. He fought wild animals. He lived through harsh hailstorms. He even said he had fourteen bullet wounds.

Eventually, Love had to stop working as a cowboy. Trains started to carry cattle across the country. People did not need a lot of cowboys anymore. So Love took a job with the railroad instead.

Rodeo Star

Bill Pickett was another famous African American cowboy. He lived from 1870 to 1932. He performed in shows called **rodeos**.

Many rodeo events are very dangerous. For instance, cowboys rope cattle and ride bulls. Pickett broke almost every bone in his body. But this did not stop him. Pickett went on to appear in two movies.

On the Range

Pickett and Love are just two people. There were thousands of famous African Americans from the Old West. Others include Cherokee Bill, Jesse Stahl, Arthur L. Walker, Ben Hodges, Mary Fields, and Rufus Buck. Some were good guys. Others were outlaws. They all helped build the West. But history has forgotten them. Why?

Left Out of the Legend

Long ago, real cowboys were stars. That changed. By the 1950s, most people learned about cowboys from popular books, movies, and TV shows. But these usually did not include African American cowboys. People started to think that all cowboys were white. The real story got lost.

Today we know better. People are remembering the forgotten cowboys. That matters. After all, African Americans helped build the Old West and America.

Wordwise

cattle: cows

Civil War: conflict in the United States between 1861 and 1865

discrimination: unequal treatment

rodeo: cowboy show

You've heard of the cowboys of the Wild West. But have you ever heard of *gauchos*? Gauchos roam the open plains of Argentina. Find out how they survive in another wild land.

By Shirleyann Costigan

El Gau

A stray cow leaves its herd. It runs across the grasslands. A man on horseback goes after it. The horse turns fast as it reaches the cow. The rider sticks like glue on the horse's back. He drives the cow back to the herd.

Welcome to the world of the gaucho. He is like the cowboy of the old western United States. He works long hours on ranches. He catches wild horses. He goes on long cattle drives. He cooks beef over an open fire. He drinks bitter *maté* tea.

The Gaucho's Trail

The life of a gaucho is hard. Yet, to many in Argentina, the gaucho is a **folk hero**. He is seen as noble and independent. Festivals celebrate his history and culture. He is a symbol of national pride.

This was not always the case. Hundreds of years ago, the gaucho was a wanderer with no home.

Over time, Argentina changed. So did the gaucho and his image. The wanderer became a soldier. The soldier became a ranch-hand. The ranch-hand became an outlaw. Finally, the outlaw became a folk hero. To see how the gaucho's image changed, let's follow his trail.

Wanderer of the Pampas

The gaucho's trail begins on the Pampas. The Pampas are grassy plains in central Argentina. Here, the flat, empty land stretches far. In the past, it took a tough person to survive here. It took a gaucho.

Still, to the gaucho, the Pampas was more than a home. It was like a mother. It gave him what he needed to survive. He hunted wild cattle and birds for food and clothing. He also caught wild horses.

The gaucho lived on his horse. He did almost everything on it. When he wasn't riding, he might say, "I am without feet."

The gaucho became known for his skills with horses. He used a saddle that had leather straps for his feet. He did not wear shoes. Instead, he held the straps between his first and second toes.

Survival Tools

The gaucho's horse helped him survive. He also used an important tool, called a *facón*, or knife. He kept it in a belt. He used it to protect himself. He also used it to kill and skin animals. He cooked their meat over an open fire. Then he used his knife like a fork to eat.

To catch animals, the gaucho used a rope called a *bola*. He made it out of three strips of animal skin. He tied a leather-covered rock to the end of each strip.

To use the bola, he circled it above his head. Faster and faster it went. Then, he let it fly. The three leather strips went around the animal's legs. Down the animal went.

To stay warm, the gaucho wore a wool blanket called a *poncho*. It also kept him dry. At night, he slept on his poncho.

Unlike the gauchos of the past, this gaucho uses stirrups and boots.

Gauchos are known for their riding skills. Here, a gaucho drives horses across a river.

From Wanderer to Soldier

Life for the early gauchos was simple. Then, in the 1800s, three important things happened. These things changed the gauchos' lives forever.

First, Argentina went to war with Spain. Spain had run Argentina for nearly 300 years. Now Argentina wanted to be independent. Gauchos became soldiers.

Their survival skills made them good fighters. They sent herds of cattle into enemy camps. They roped Spanish soldiers. When under attack, they hid in the grasslands.

From War Hero to Ranch-Hand

The gauchos helped win a war. They also won respect. More ranchers began hiring gauchos. After all, they didn't need much. They were tough as nails. And they were fine cowboys.

In the early 1800s, the plains were wide open. **Descendants** of Spanish settlers built large *estancias*, or ranches. They marked their fields with trees and ditches. Their cattle wandered freely. So did the gauchos. Then another big change came in the 1840s. It changed ranch life. It also changed the gauchos' lives.

This couple keeps gaucho tradition alive with a special dance.

From Ranch-Hand to Outlaw

The change came after one rancher visited England. He saw how fences made it easier to raise **livestock** with fewer workers. He brought that idea back to Argentina. Soon, ranchers began making fences.

Immigrants from Europe moved to the Pampas. They began farming. They built fences, too. Over time, the open spaces went away.

Their world was changing. But the gauchos tried to stay the same. The ranchers didn't understand the gauchos. They said the gauchos took animals from their land. The gaucho got a new name: outlaw.

From Outlaw to Hero

Few people respected these outlaws. Then the gauchos' image changed again. In the 1870s, a poet wrote a long poem called "El gaucho Martín Fierro." It described one gaucho's life. It told how he loved freedom more than things. It told how he had been treated badly.

Many Argentines read the poem. They loved Fierro's independent spirit. They admired his goodness. Once again, the Argentine people respected the gaucho. His life was still hard. Yet now he was a hero, not an outlaw. And so the legend of the gaucho was born.

Gauchos Today

Today, there are still gauchos in Argentina. They may drive a truck. They may live in a house. Some still work on ranches. Others have found jobs in cities.

Yet they keep the gaucho traditions alive. They do it with songs, poems, and dances. Gauchos show their skills at rodeos and festivals. They rope cattle. They ride wild horses. They do traditional dances.

Meanwhile, deep in the Pampas, some gauchos still wander. Like their fathers and grandfathers, they live off the land. They hold on to the old ways.

Can they survive in modern Argentina? No one knows. But one thing is certain. The gauchos will fight to keep their traditions alive.

A son am I of the rolling plain
A gaucho born and bred,
And this is my pride: to live as free
As the bird that cuts through the sky.
from "El gaucho Martín Fierro"

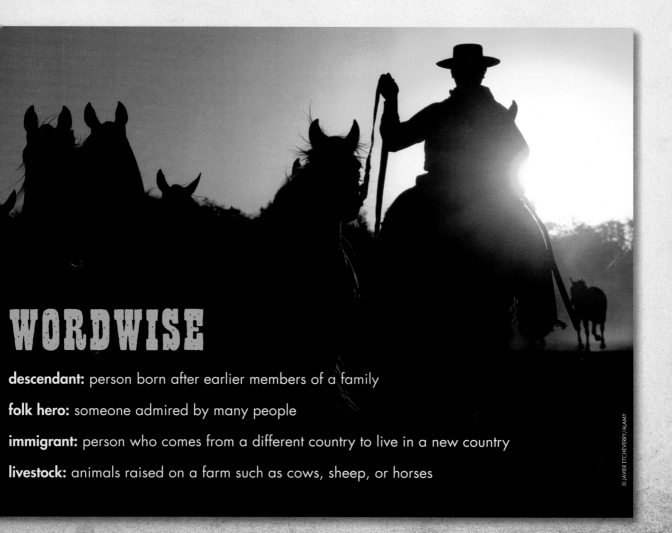

WORDWISE

descendant: person born after earlier members of a family

folk hero: someone admired by many people

immigrant: person who comes from a different country to live in a new country

livestock: animals raised on a farm such as cows, sheep, or horses

© JAVIER ETCHEVERRY/ALAMY

COWBOYS

What did you learn about cowboys?
Answer these questions to find out.

1 Why did many African Americans move west after the Civil War?

2 How did books, movies, and television change people's image of cowboys in the United States?

3 Why were gauchos good soldiers?

4 Picture a gaucho. What does he look like? What is he doing?

5 What is "wild" about a cowboy's life?